REMINISCENCES

OF

REAR ADMIRAL CLARENCE E. OLSEN
U. S. NAVY (RETIRED)

AS THEY PERTAIN TO THE

YALTA CONFERENCE

U. S. NAVAL INSTITUTE
ANNAPOLIS, MARYLAND
1972

This is a single interview given by Rear Admiral Clarence E. Olsen, U. S. Navy (Retired) to John T. Mason, Jr., at the U. S. Naval Institute on June 23, 1970.

The manuscript has been corrected by Admiral Olsen for minor errors but the reader is reminded that it remains the spoken word rather than the written word.

Excerpts from a letter of Admiral Olsen to Mrs. Olsen under date of January 19, 1944 are attached in the form of an appendix. The letter was an immediate and first-hand account of the Yalta episode.

DECLARATION OF TRUST

The undersigned does hereby appoint and designate as his (her) Trustee herein, the Secretary-Treasurer and Publisher of the United States Naval Institute to perform and discharge the following duties, powers, and privileges in connection with the possession and use of a certain taped interview between the undersigned and the Oral History Department of the United States Naval Institute.

1. Classification of Transcript.

(X)a. If classified OPEN, the transcript(s) may be read or the recording(s) audited by the qualified personnel upon presentation of proper credentials, as determined by the Secretary-Treasurer of the U. S. Naval Institute.

( )b. If classified PERMISSION REQUIRED TO CITE OR QUOTE, the user will be required to obtain permission in writing from the interviewee prior to quoting or citing from either the transcript(s) or the recording(s).

( )c. If classified PERMISSION REQUIRED, permission must be obtained in writing from the interviewee before the transcribed interview(s) can be examined or the tape recording(s) audited.

( )d. If classified CLOSED, the transcribed interview(s) and the tape recording(s) will be sealed until a time specified by the interviewee. This may be until the death of the interviewee or for any specified number of years.

2. It is expressly understood that in giving this authorization, I am in no way precluded from placing such restrictions as I may desire upon use of the interview at any time during my lifetime, nor does this authorization in any way affect my rights to the copyright of my literary expressions that may be contained in the interview.

Witness my hand and seal this 29th day of August 19 76

I hereby accept and consent to the foregoing Declaration of Trust and the powers therein conferred upon me as Trustee:

Interview with Rear Admiral Clarence E. Olsen

Place: U. S. Naval Institute, Annapolis, Maryland

Date: Tuesday afternoon, 23 June 1970

Subject: Tour of Duty in Moscow, World War II

By: John T. Mason, Jr.

Q: Admiral, it's a delight to meet you. Ever since I heard about you the other night from Kemp Tolley, I've been anxious to meet you and I've been preparing for it by doing a little reading for background purposes.

Since we can meet only this one time, I wonder if you would start out, perhaps, by telling me about your service in Washington on the staff of Admiral King, which was in 1942-43?

Adm. O.: I came to Washington from duty out on the West Coast as a member of the planning staff under Admiral Cooke, and served there for about twenty months before I was sent over to Moscow. My duties there were quite general. Nothing very specific concerning Russia, except in one instance where we were making a study of the Northern Passage. They asked me to collect all the data that I could and prepare a paper to show what the prospects of developing the Northern Passage might be.

Q: This is beyond Murmansk?

Adm. O.: This is up north from Japan, around northern Russia to Murmansk.

I prepared that paper and it was passed in to Admiral

Cooke and Admiral King and so forth, and from there on, as far as I know, it was forgotten, because I never heard anything more about it, until, towards the end of my time, I was due to go to sea to the West Coast to take command of a division of APAs, when one Sunday morning I was called in by Admiral Bieri and asked to give him some advice on several of my classmates as to their qualifications for the job in Moscow.

Q: I know him quite well, having talked to him for the last couple of years.

Adm. O.: He named one and I had a premonition that I was involved in there, but he assured me that I was not. Those people that were due to go to sea were exempt, and he had Admiral Edwards' assurance that I was exempt. So that made me feel free to express myself a little more freely.

Q: Did you have any knowledge of the Russian language or anything of that sort?

Adm. O.: No. I didn't even know where Moscow was.

Q: But I suppose that was also true of your classmates.

Adm. O.: It certainly was. So I gave him my opinions and he selected the man who was going over to relieve Admiral Duncan. They told me why Duncan was coming out, primarily, I suspected, because the ambassador was not going to be able to go back...

Q: Standley?

Adm. O.: Standley....since he had forced the Russians to admit that they were getting all this Lend-Lease material, and that it was true that they were changing all the labels on the packages and so forth, and telling their people that this was American goods that they'd paid high prices for, and so forth. In other words, he forced them to lose face, and when he came home about that time, I think he had a firm conviction that he wasn't going to be allowed to get back, which was apparently true.

Q: Was he anxious to go back, anyway?

Adm. O.: I don't think he wanted any part of it.

Q: I don't think so. That's the impression I had.

Adm. O.: Anyway, they selected Ambassador Harriman - Averell Harriman - to replace him, and at that time they decided to send in a military mission instead of having the naval attache...

Q: What was the reason for that?

Adm. O.: That I don't know. I was not in the Joint Chiefs of Staff conference that decided that, and all I know is that they selected General Deane, who was then a brigadier, as the head of the mission and, since they were just making him a major general for this purpose, he was junior to Admiral Duncan, who had been an admiral for a couple of years. Therefore, Duncan had to come out. Somebody else had to go in. That was the reason for this sudden flail. So I went back to my office and came back to the shop the next day, Monday, and the first thing I knew, my buzzer rang, and I walked in to Admiral Cooke's office, and he got up and said, "Congratulations, Commodore!" I said, "You can't do this to me. I'm going to the Pacific." He said, "You've got three days to change your uniforms, pack your bags, and go with the Secretary to Moscow."

Q: Admiral Bieri knew this?

Adm. O.: Bieri was sitting right there and all he could do was hide his head in shame. So I went home and got my wife back from Michigan, packed my bags, and got all my credentials and so forth, and I was in the plane at sunrise on Thursday morning on my way to Moscow.

Q: How did your wife react to this?

Adm. O.: She naturally didn't like it, because she was just coming in from three months' vacation up in Michigan and, fortunately, she was coming back that Monday evening, anyway. So when I told her what was in the wind, I broke it rather brusquely because riding back from the plane, I said, "How would you like to sleep with a commodore tonight?" She reached over and started to poke me and then suddenly said, "What!"

Q: She realized...

Adm. O.: She realized the significane of it, and I said, "Yes, I'm appointed to special duty and I'm on my way to Moscow."

Q: Wives weren't included?

Adm. O.: Wives definitely were not included at that time. Harriman had his daughter over there and they had several girl secretaries, and the Minister later on that came in had his wife there, but that was all. Others were excluded.

So we went in and I stayed for the duration of the conference with the State Department...

Q: What kind of briefing had you received in preparation for this?

Adm. O.: None. Absolutely none. I spent two days there trying to find out a few things. Fortunately, Admiral Duncan was in town. He had come back with Admiral Standley, and I could get ahold of him for a few wise words about clothing and supplies and things like that, how to handle your money affairs, but I had no time to learn the language but did manage to buy a book on the language. I had no time for any real briefing of the circumstances over there. So I went in cold.

Q: It might have been wise....

Adm. O.: It would have helped a little bit I think, but then Duncan went back over there and was with me for two weeks. That was a great help.

Q: That was your indoctrination!

Adm. O.: That was my real indoctrination. Later I traveled to learn more. Of course, you know, we had Sam Frankel up in Murmansk as our senior representative there...

Q: He was quite effective, wasn't he?

Adm. O.: He was cracker jack. He spoke fluent Russian and they all liked him. He liked the job and he did a splendid job on handling those ships that came in on the convoys so completely damaged. He did a whale of a job trying to convince the Russians to repair the ships, but this was impossible. Nobody could do that because they didn't have the materials, nor the time to waste repairing American ships. As a result they cannibalized several of the ships to make possible the repair of others and get them out, and those that were cannibalized just stayed there until such time as we officially turned them over to the Russians for nothing - part of Lend Lease.

Q: Were many Russian merchant vessels involved in these convoys to Murmansk?

Adm. O.: No. No Russian vessels. They were all American and British.

Q: And no Russian escorts, either?

Adm. O.: All American and British escorts. Of course, immediately after we turned the dead ships over to the Russians, they moved them out and turned to and repaired them and had them running on their own in a reasonably short time.

Q: Facilities in Murmansk were quite limited, anyway, weren't they?

Adm. O.: Very limited. There's no question. We can't blame

the Russians too much for the way they looked at things, because they were in desperation all the time. They had practically nothing and they didn't have too good leadership. They didn't have anybody who had any idea of organization or planning on these things. They just drove ahead and did the best they could with what they could get their hands on...

Q: And innately suspicious of any foreign adviser!

Adm. O.: They were suspicious, but they were always there with their hands out for more. Sam was great in helping them out all he could, and I think that he got as much from them as was humanly possible under the circumstances. And he was up there for almost four years. In fact, I had a hard time convincing him that, much as I wanted to keep him there, for his own future career it was fatal if he stayed, and I urged him to come out, which he finally concurred in. I recommended to ONI that he be sent to the Pacific and be given an intelligence job related to Japan and Russia in a standby status for future use in case we had to go in up there. Fortunately, that's what they did with him, and at one time, I know, he was slated to go on into Russia, but the proposition fell through, unnecessary and so forth, so he did not actually go in. But he was there, and I gather he did a whale of a good job on everything else he did out there because he eventually became the first admiral in intelligence, and became head of ONI.

Q: Oh, did he?

Adm. O.: Oh, yes.

Q: I remember him being at Murmansk when I was in ONI, too, during the war. I didn't realize that he went on to be...

Adm. O.: Oh, yes, he was head of ONI for two years or more.

Q: Let me ask, did you go to Murmansk yourself very often?

Adm. O.: I went up there, I think three times - three or four times. Twice in the winter months, which was very rugged because the train service was bad and part of it we had to finish in one of their propeller-driven snow sleds because the train got stalled.

Q: What kind of temperatures were you involved in?

Adm. O.: Oh, the temperatures were down below zero - five or ten degrees below zero - most of the time. I visited a number of the ships that were tied up at the dock there, and talked with the skippers and so forth - talked about arrangements. I saw the kind of labor that they got, which was all prison labor being marched from barracks to dock at the point of guns and at the end of bayonets.

Q: Political prisoners, were they?

Adm. O.: These were all political prisoners or helpless people who were being forced to do the labor of unloading. Of course, they were all starved, emaciated. All they had on their bodies, outside of a few clothes, was a tin cup lashed to their belt, which was what they ate and drank from, and washed their teeth, if they ever did. It was not uncommon for them to be carrying, say, a case of lard down the gangway of the docks and they would inadvertently drop it so that it would burst wide open and a can or two would break open and they'd all dive in there with their hands and just dig it out with their fingers - eat just plain lard, cold, as fast as they could to get the fat, get the grease.

Q: Starving for fat. Were men and women involved in this?

Adm. O.: Men and women, both. Yes, it didn't make any difference to the Russians. And, in one case, when I was up there, the ships were all frozen in. Of course, they emptied their garbage out through the slop shate on the fantail, right out on the ice. One of these prisoners couldn't stand it when he saw all this bread and potato peelings and things like that going down on the ice. He just jumped out of ranks, jumped onto the ice and began to scoop it up with both hands. A guard just picked up his gun and shot him through the head and left him there. Sam had a hell of a time then for I don't know how many days persuading them to remove the body. They just wanted it to stay there as an example to the rest of the troops that were working on storage and so forth.

Q: Were they housed in barracks, or what?

Adm. O.: I never saw that, but they were housed in some sort of old barns, buildings, back in the backwoods, unheated, of course, and slabs of wood laid out there to sleep on, and I suppose...

Q: Well, that must have been somewhat disheartening to the seamen on American and British vessels to witness this...

Adm. O.: They were thoroughly disgusted. In fact, I heard repeatedly that the sailors were so disgusted with it that they swore they would never go on another convoy to Russia. I think they had trouble with recruiting in some instances after that, because of what the sailors had brought back home.

Q: It was exceedingly difficult convoy duty, anyway, wasn't it?

Adm. O.: They were the worst convoy duties in the whole world in any war that we've ever had, I think, because they were sitting ducks going up around the North Cape there, for the German submarines and for the German air. Some of those convoys came in, not decimated, but almost obliterated. Half of them would be sunk or destroyed, and others would be just crippled to the point where they could barely creep in. I don't remember exact numbers, but I'd say an average of about half of them got through.

Q: Did the Russian officials not have some understanding of the psychological effect this would have on foreigners?

Adm. O.: I don't think they had any idea of that and it meant nothing to them. Lives to them meant nothing at all. They're just absolutely cold-blooded. This was exemplified all through the war, the way they piled bodies up in front of cities and drove the people in over the minefields and that sort of thing, in order to clear the way for the troops coming afterwards. Life just meant nothing to them. Their objective was what they were after, no matter how much life they lost. It was always to gain the objective.

Q: How did this affect you as a person? I mean being suddenly thrust into this situation?

Adm. O.: I tried not to worry about it because there was nothing we could do about it. It made us thoroughly disgusted, of course, but there was nothing we could do about it, except appreciate the fact that the Russians were doing everything they could to get the most out of people.

Q: What other ports were involved in the Lend-Lease program?

Adm. O.: Arkhangelsk and Molotorsk. We had a small group there under a lieutenant. And Vladivostok, where we had Commander Roulard, a chief yeoman, and his interpreter. His was primarily a duty of intelligence reporting until later on some of the shipments of relief stores came through Vladivostok and then came by train on to Moscow. Otherwise, there was practically nothing about the war that he had to worry about.

Q: Did you visit that port?

Adm. O.: No. I sent one of my captains out there to visit with him one time. That meant ten days on the train going over and ten days coming back, and I didn't think that I could be spared for a month during these times, so -

Q: Terribly rigorous, too!

Adm. O.: It's not fun because you're on a train all the time and living in one small compartment. You have to bring all your own food, and all your own liquid supplies, of course. About the only thing they furnished was hot water for tea. So that it was a rigorous trip.

Q: Were the cars heated?

Adm. O.: The compartments were partially heated, but not much. You were usually wrapped in heavy clothes, and you slept in most of them! I made the trip up to Murmansk - two trips up there by train that way, and then I made the trip down to Yalta that way, and they were all very uncomfortable trips. But they were an experience because every time you came to a railroad station, you saw things that you wouldn't believe. People crowding in with great big burlap bags of clothing and supplies. Lord only knows where they were going to, but everybody wanted to move, it seemed. When the train pulled out, not only was every car just packed standing room, but they were up on the roof of the train, and all over it. The train pulled out with them even hanging by the handrails, and they would hang on there till their hands froze or they got so cold they just dropped off. Of course, the train was only going about 15 miles an hour, anyway, so it wasn't much of a serious drop. But they just wanted to move on toward their destinatio

Q: Were they leaving areas that were threatened with invasion or something?

Adm. O.: At the time - the principal time I speak of was going

Olsen - 13

down to Yalta. I think they were returning there after the German occupation. I can't imagine why else there was this great crowd moving south, unless they wanted to get warm weather.

Q: That might be a real incentive!

Adm. O.: Yes.

Q: You say that Admiral Standley had had some words with the Russian officials about proper labeling of the Lease Lend items. During your time there, did they attend to this and give us fair credit?

Adm. O.: As far as we knew, after that everything was sent down marked with U. S. shipping labels and signs just as they came in. Whether it was changed near the front or not, I never knew, but we never had any words with them about it.

Q: What was involved in Lease Lend at this particular time?

Adm. O.: Oh, everything in the world you could think of. All kinds of ammunition, food, medical supplies, trucks, automobiles in general, airplane parts. The list that they would give us for requests was almost unbelievable. As a matter of fact, at times it was ridiculous, and we, of course, through our Lend Lease office there, had to screen a lot of these things to try to cut them down to something normal. For instance, when the Milwaukee came in up north (she was the only large ship we gave them under lend lease), they gave us a list of replacement parts up there that would sink the ship. We pointed out to them that the ship had been completely overhauled in New York before it came over there. They had all modern radio and radar equipment and things, the latest one, allowed for that type, the storerooms were full with a year and a half of supplies, and yet three months later they were requesting enough supplies to sink the ship. It was obvious - they wanted to winterize the ship, they said, and build houses over it. Well, you can't keep a man of war in shape by putting everything under cover. But they claimed the ship wasn't built for the cold-weather service that they had up north, which was just another of their "come-ons." It was quite obvious that they weren't interested in rebuilding or supplying the Milwaukee. They were just interested in an excuse to get everything they could lay their hands on for other purposes.

Q: It wasn't a degree of naievete, then?

Adm. O.: It was just plain, blunt demand without any excuse or reason, or any cover at all. Just blunt demand for a lot of things. In fact, at one time, Admiral Kuznetsov, the commander-in-chief of the Navy, had me in for a conference as he wanted a number of minelayers assigned to the Russian Navy. I believe the number was 114, if I remember, and I said, "Well, Admiral, that is a large request." He said, "We have a great requirement in all of our areas for these minelayers. I said, "But, Admiral, I think that you know obviously from the number that you are requesting, that that includes the entire shipbuilding program in that category of the U. S. Navy, that only one-third of it is complete now, and the rest of it won't be complete for another year or more." He said, "But we need every one of them." I said, "There are only about seven other battle areas which need them also and it is the duty of the Joint Chiefs of Staff to determine how many go to each area." He says, "They don't need them in the other areas like we need them here. The Bear has a voracious appetite." I said, "I agree with that. I'm sorry I can't agree with your request for 114 minelayers." And he said, "We want all we can get." So I said, "I'll transmit your request to the Joint Chiefs of Staff with my recommendations." I think I recommended five or something like that. But I mean they had no hesitancy about asking for the impossible. That was only one instance where they did that.

In another they requested that I get for them detailed plans and specifications of all of our types of Navy ships, from carriers on down to harbor craft. I almost laughed at them, but you can't do that to a four-star admiral, and I asked them why they had a need for that. They said, well, they're going to build. I said, "But you can't build any of these things during the war years, so that's a postwar requirement and not - current requirement." But they said, there will be great efforts made to increase our Navy after the war, and we need these plans. I said, "Admiral, you haven't got a chance in a million to get those plans, because you have no current need for them. If I submit this request, I'm afraid that my CNO will just laugh at the whole thing, but if you wish,

Olsen - 16

I will send it in." I sent it in with my own comments and recommendation and, of course, nothing else ever came of it. But that was the character of the people. They would demand or request, unlimited things, without any reason or logical backing for it.

Q: Was that the character of officialdom, or would you say generally it was the character of the whole people?

Adm. O.: Oh, not of the people. The officialdom was the whole thing in this case. No, the people themselves were hungry for what they could get, of course, but they had no relation to these Lend Lease programs. It was just their official demand to supply their army and their navy and their air force. The Army ran into the same thing, and General Spaulding and Gen. Faymanvill before him, had a very difficult time screening out what was reasonable and what was unreasonable. (Gens. Spaulding and Faymanvill headed up the lend lease end of the program in Russia.)

Q: Were they at a stage where they could see the dawn and feel that they would survive the German onslaught, so they were out to get what they could when they could?

Adm. O.: I wouldn't quite say that, because they were never clear or sure of victory until after Stalingrad. You see, after Moscow and after Stalingrad and after the liberation of Leningrad, then they began to move and to see some hope for the future, after they had driven the Germans out of southern Russia and out of the Stalingrad area. So it wasn't all that. They were absolutely strapped. There was no denying that they didn't have but a very limited amount of

their own resources and they had depleted everything in Russia
from Vladivostok on east, including personnel. I went out to
the city of Gorky, about 150 miles east of Moscow - one time,
as the guest of the general who was their chief - a hydrographer.
He seemed to develop a more close friendship with us than some
of the others, he was more or less nonmilitary. At Gorky they
had automobile factories and other plants, but the only people
we saw around the streets were children, old women - or women -
and very old men. Very, very few men. No young men or really
healthy young people visible anywhere. Everything had been
taken out and moved up to the front. And in their movements
from Moscow west, well, as you have probably read in their
history, they cannibalized every city that they went through,
took all the able-bodied personnel and marched them toward the
front, trained them with the guns as they went forward, and when
they got to the front, they were supposed to be trained, having
marched for five days or something like that, and they were the
buffer for the regular troops. That's how little they cared
for lives.

Q: Their own!

Adm. O.: Their own lives. They didn't care how many they
lost so long as they gained the objective. And, as you know
from their history, too, they usually planned and accumulated
enough gunnery, artillery and so forth, stockpiled outside
to be three or four times what normally a commander would
actually need or want before they struck. Because when
they struck they wanted to annihilate, and they usually did.

They wanted to make damned sure of their success, and that was one way of doing it, by stockpiling until they were sure they had enough to go through with it - or more than enough. Those are characteristics of their leadership.

Q: How crucial would you say, then, was our Lease Lend effort to them in this time of great need?

Adm. O.: Oh, without it they never could have accomplished anything to speak of such as they did.

Q: Did they ever admit this?

Adm. O.: Oh, heavens, no. No, they never admitted to their people that they had gotten any successful great help from the United States. But it was absolutely evident everywhere you went. General Deane, I think, had more opportunity to see this up at the front than any of us because we were never allowed to go up to the front. He did on several occasions with the Army generals. He went up there with General Antonoff, I think, and Zhukov and others. I think he mentioned in his book Strange Alliance several instances when he went up there.

Q: Another aspect of your job was to have an exchange of weather information. Was this a difficult thing to achieve?

Adm. O.: Not very, since we supplied all of the equipment and in the China area of the north Siberian area, we provided personnel to help them install these things, but they would never allow us to man stations. They wanted everything provided to them and get their instructions and so forth, which we gave them in Moscow, and also in the Far East, then they wanted to set them up themselves and run them.

Q: Were they adept...?

Adm. O.: They were quite capable. They had a very good weather office there. I can't think of the general's name now who was head of it. His captain assistant was Spranski, but the general's name I can't think of. But I think that they helped us out a great deal because we were able to feed weather information to our fleet in the Pacific which helped them in their flights from the various stations in the fleet up into the Japan area. You see, we had no other sources of weather information coming from the North and West of our Pacific forces, and weather in that area moved from Siberia toward the Pacific. And so what they got from the Russians was all they got. I would evaluate that as a very helpful service.

Q: Why did the Russians not want any of our personnel to be involved in transmitting information?

Adm. O.: They didn't want anybody - any foreigner - over there for any reason at all. We were only in Moscow on tolerance. But they did not want foreigners in their country. That was almost a positive rule. They would not allow anybody to operate in their country.

Q: Just an innate suspicion.

Adm. O.: Always suspicious. When we set up the three airfields in the south there to facilitate the straight-over bombing from England and Italy, straight across and landing in Russia to refuel and rebomb and then fly back...

Q: Was that the bombing raids on Ploesti and all that?

Adm. O.: Yes, that area...we had a very difficult time justifying our personnel.

Q: They couldn't see this as a strategic operation that was necessary and helping them?

Adm. O.: Yes, they realized it would help, but they were always suspicious that we had an ulterior motive. The suspicion that goes on in their minds is something unbelievable.

Q: Have you ever tried to analyze the root of this? Why is it?

Adm. O.: No. I really don't know the answer to that.

Q: It must have been awfully frustrating dealing with people when they're always suspecting you of having other motives!

Adm. O.: Our operations were always handicapped because we would give them information freely, all that we had that was going to be helpful. We on the other hand would have some things we wanted their assistance on. We'd go into a conference with them and have this all written out, laid it on the line, said we would like this and like that, like you to do this in order to facilitate such and such an operation. And the answer

Olsen - 21

would always be they'd take it into consideration and would let you know in a day or two. Well, you'd prod them on for another meeting because you wanted the answers as quickly as you could get them, and, finally, after several delays, they would call you in for a conference and then they would tell you that this isn't necessary because we've already done this. See, they would take our things and our information and what we wanted and they would implement everything they could to practically make any further advice or information to us unnecessary.

Q: And they used this delay to...

Adm. O.: They used the delay to accomplish everything that they could to forestall having to do anything more with us. And that happened time and time again. Of course, it served a purpose in one way in getting some things done, but it blocked us in a thousand ways in getting information which we needed to carry out our part of operations. But that was, again, their suspicious attitude. They didn't want us to take credit or get credit for anything.

Q: And during your period there of two years, did you see any improvement in this situation, or did it always remain the same?

Adm. O.: It was pretty much the same from start to finish. It was a built-in characteristic. It was no use to fight it. Citing one instance: I was there as head when Deane went to

England right at the end of the war. Our troops were crossing Germany and Eisenhower had told - they had an agreement that our troops would go up to the Oder River and the Russians would meet us there. Well, actually, our troops overran the river by about 40-odd miles, and during that time we were trying to make agreements on signals and signs so that the Russians would recognize our tanks and our troops as American rather than German. During that time we were collaborating quite closely with them. Then Eisenhower sent a dispatch to General Antonoff saying that after contact was made with the Soviet troops moving westward, the American troops would move back to this agreed river line.

I delivered this dispatch to General Antonoff and his staff about 2 o'clock in the morning and he just looked at me, and he asked that I read it over again. I agreed - through an interpreter, of course - and then he looked at me and said, "Did General Eisenhower send this?" I said, "Yes, of course he sent it." "How do you know he sent it?" "I had no question in my mind that he had sent it." He said, "Would you go back to your office and send and ask General Eisenhower for a confirmation of this statement?" They wouldn't believe that anybody would be so foolish as to back down 40 miles over captured land. As a result, I went back and sent back to General Eisenhower and asked, told him General Antonoff requested confirmation of dispatch so-and-so. It came back almost immediately, and at 5 o'clock in the morning I was back there with the confirmation. He thanked me very much, then they went ahead and did what they wanted to do, moving their troops forward to meet ours and pushed back to the river.

On first delivery, the Russian mind just could not believe that any advancing general would give up captured land, which again is characteristic of them. You know perfectly well if the Russians had gone 40 miles the other side of the Oder, towards us, that they never would have backed down. We'd have had a hell of a fight with them to make them back down!

Q: Were the British involved in any Lease Lend operations, too?

Adm. O.: Yes, but to a lesser extent, mostly through our offices.

Q: Routed through our facilities? Yes, I see.

Adm. O.: They had a staff over there, of course, but it was relatively small. And a lot of our material went through England, and was transshipped. It came to England and then was reloaded into the convoys forming there and shipped up north.

Q: And they had the same kind of treatment on the part of the Russian officials?

Adm. O.: The Russians, I'm afraid, treated the British far worse than they ever treated us. They just didn't like the British. They had a very, very deep hatred of the British. The British invaded up there, you know, at Murmansk in World War I.

Q: Yes. When Lenin was trying to take over.

Olsen - 24

Adm. O.: Yes, and they have never forgotten! In fact, once a British general, when he came to Moscow, boasted out loud at cocktail parties that he had been in the troops that had landed up north at that time. He was under suspicion from then on. He couldn't go anywhere from then on and he finally left. I think they asked him to leave. They didn't like the British at all. I could confirm that by several experiences, but we won't go into that for the record.

Q: Would you tell me, since one of your very important duties was to make all the necessary arrangements for the Yalta conference - would you tell me about that in some detail?

Adm. O.: Well, I wish I could find the letter that I wrote to my wife during that month because we were not allowed to send anything out from Yalta, and so I just took a large yellow pad, such as you've got there, and each day I wrote my thoughts and events of the day in letter form, and then after we got out I rolled it up in a packet like a newspaper and sent it to her - not quite that voluminous, but in there I had all the details. I can remember quite a bit of it, but if I could only find that some time I think it would make an interesting story to write up. [I found it later.]

Q: It would be an historic document, I must say. Had you kept a diary while you were there?

Adm. O.: No. We were not supposed to do that. This running diary that I kept while I was there, illegal as it was, I did keep because I knew that this was an occasion where - a historic occasion - I'd never have another opportunity to experience.

Q: Just a kind of a footnote, were our facilities for sending letters home and documents, were they sacrosanct? I mean, was there a diplomatic pouch?

Adm. O.: We went through the Embassy pouches and outside of a plane or two shot down now and then, we had no problems at all.

Q: There was courier service?

Adm. O.: Courier service. I sent all of my pay checks, for instance, and all the rest of us did, too, sent them back to the mainland to the bank or to our wives, properly endorsed, through the Embassy mail. I never lost a check in the 20 months I was over there.

Q: Incidentally, how was living there? I mean, was it pleasant enough, or was it very rigorous?

Adm. O.: Yes, well, we all had apartments provided by the Embassy at the tolerance of the Russians.

Q: In the compound, or...?

Adm. O.: No. Our Embassy building was right near the
National Hotel and the Kremlin, where the ambassador's offices
were. His living quarters, Spasso House, was quite a way off,
about a mile or two, but most of us lived in the housing
section of the embassy staff buildings, their office buildings.
They were reasonably well furnished and heated up to about
60 degrees during the winter time, conservative on their heat,
as about everything else. Food, we got some through the local
market, but most of it we got as excess American supplies
from the survivors' stores that had been shipped in to help
the shipping up at Murmansk to survive through the winter
and so forth. And once that pipeline was filled, it was hard
to stop it, so even long after there was no need for it, these
supplies kept coming in from various sources, five, ten,
fifteen tons at a time, until I had something well over a
hundred tons of supplies stashed away, including heavy weather
clothing and so forth. So I got the Navy Department's permission to re-sell what was needed to the Embassy to establish
a commissary, which really saved our necks and made
living very reasonable, and the feed was much better than we
could ever do on the public market. Public market food was
terribly expensive. Eggs were, for instance, a dollar a piece
and were usually rotten when you got them. Meat was terrifi-
cally high priced.

Q: How did the ordinary Russian...?

Adm. O.: They lived on potatoes and cabbage and black bread,
mostly. With a little vodka when they could get it.

Q: Was that fairly inexpensive, vodka?

Adm. O.: Vodka was inexpensive. The Russian physique was not really good. They were - a doctor pointed out that on this limited diet, they were usually anemic to some extent, so they didn't have the strength, the stamina, that they would normally have on an adequate protein diet. But we were pretty well supplied. Then after the end of the war in Europe, when we had these prisoners all coming back through Russia and moving down to Odessa, where the Army established a camp for them...

Q: German prisoners?

Adm. O.: No, American prisoners. They had escaped or were released from out of the prison camps and a lot of them moved into Russia instead of going through Germany, thinking that would be the best way to get out. The Russians just put them on flat cars or box cars in the middle of the winter and moved them on down to Odessa. They had very little food and clothing there, so I...

Q: They were treating them the way they treated their own nationals.

Adm. O.: Naturally, because they didn't have any provision for their own people either. I went to the ambassador and pointed out that I had all these supplies, and with his concurrence I sent over a hundred tons of supplies down to the camp in Odessa to help feed and support and clothe our own prisoners there until they could get out on ships.

Q: were our Army people doing likewise?

Adm. O.: I was the only one that had the total supplies - the survivors' stores.

Q: That was all Navy?

Adm. O.: Yes, but I tell you the Army was mighty glad to get it, because they had very little other source of supply at the time, other than what they could arrange to ship in themselves. So that was a means of closing up the pipeline of survivors' stores coming in and putting a good practical use to it for our own people.

Q: Did Spasso House exist on that ration, too?

Adm. O.: They got their own share, you bet your life!

Q: And maybe more?

Adm. O.: No rations. But going back to the other thing, if I could just make a brief summary of some of the things there, and then if I ever get into my files and can find this other, I might write the thing up for you, in detail.

Q: Oh, good.

Adm. O.: But as you know from your history, this thing started before Christmas in 1944 when Roosevelt was asking Stalin about a meeting, and Stalin said that he would meet him any time, any place, but Roosevelt didn't want to do it until after

January, and where would he like?

Q: Roosevelt had a little thing like the election to take care of!

Adm. O.: That's right. That was correct. And Roosevelt's first dispatches to us indicated to make preparations for a group of about 35, a very small select group with himself and the Joint Chiefs of Staff and so forth, and wanted to know where Stalin would meet. So Stalin told the ambassador that he would meet in Odessa. Well, we all got rather excited about that, because Odessa was within easy bombing range of the German front lines and also Odessa was one of the most heavily mined areas in the Black Sea, and we felt that if we were going to have any kind of a conference, all of us having attended several at various times before and knowing how - what heavy demands for communications and supplies and soforth there are at that time, we figured we were going to have to have a communications ship in there.

Q: Had you been at Teheran or at Cairo?

Adm. O.: I was at Quebec, and then I was Cairo, and then at Yalta, yes.

So we told the ambassador that Odessa looked like a very poor place, from several points of view; i.e. that the Germans were within striking distance; that we couldn't get a communication ship in there; and, that in the winter weather with the cold winds coming across the steppes toward Odessa was no place to put Roosevelt in his weakened condition.

Q: And it had to be Russia?

Adm. O.: Stalin wouldn't go out of Russia. We tried to get him to go to Malta, but he wouldn't go out of Russia. He wouldn't dare go out of Russia. He suggested any place on the Black Sea Russian shore.

Q: He did go to Teheran.

Adm. O.: That's the only time, yes. He went to Teheran, but he didn't want to go into the Mediterranean. Roosevelt told him he would meet him any time, any place. Stalin had the option, then.

Q: Why was he afraid to go out of Russia?

Adm. O.: He said his doctors would not allow it because of the long flight time.

Q: But this was a fact?

Adm. O.: We had to assume that. I also think he feared oing out of Russia for security reasons. Again, their natural suspicion of everything and everybody. So Harriman told me to make a study and work with the Soviet Navy to select a better place. It was a pretty hard job because all i had was a Baedeker Guide to go by on the climate down there. I finally took it up with Admiral Kuznetsov and he agreed that Yalta would probably be the best alternate place, but they wanted time. He didn't know where they could actually get together at Yalta because it had been heavily bombed and destroyed by the Germans.

Q: It had to be a port?

Adm. O.: We wanted a port in order to get a communications ship in there. You see, they would not allow any of our communications and we had no over-air way of bringing, communications systems in adequately to meet the demands of the conference. So we wanted a ship, if possible. So, we finally agreed on Yalta. Well, that was past Christmas time then. So Harriman told me to take three officers, General Hill from the Air Force, and Ronnie Allen, my interpreter, as secretary, and Lieutenant Chase - the four of us to go down there. Allen and Chase spoke fluent Russian. Hill and I just a few smatterings of it. Stalin and Molotov approved of our going down. We were to assist them in planning this thing. Then they wouldn't give me any transportation. Day after day I appealed to them about giving me transportation down, and meanwhile the dispatches indicated that instead of having 35 they would have about 85. And the next thing we knew, they had about 125. On the final thing we had about 180 coming down.

Q: Why were they reluctant to give transportation? I mean, they wanted this conference, didn't they?

Adm. O.: Stalin did, yes. I found out afterwards that all the buildings they were going to use were in such complete disrepair after the German evacuation that they needed time to make any of them habitable in any form, and I suppose the same would have been true in Odessa if we'd gone there, but it was certainly true in Yalta. The place they chose was the Czar Nicholas' "Livadia," which had three main buildings and several minor buildings in a large compound, and had been occupied by the Germans. In fact, the Germans used the ground floor for stables for their horses, and when they pulled out of there they wrecked everything they could. They dug up the floors, they pounded down the walls, the broke all the glassware, the windows and everything. Fortunately, they did not break up the heating system. And so the Russians were busy trying to resurrect the two main buildings and needed time. One they weren't planning to resurrect until I got there and persuaded them to, but by the time I got down there in the second week of January, they had relaid all the floors, plastered up all the walls, repaired all the windows, and the heating system was operating. They were still working night and day. They had about 500 Rumanian prisoners around the grounds repairing and planting shrubbery and all that sort of thing, making the grounds presentable, in addition to several hundred working on the buildings.

Q: Before the German occupation, what had it been used for?

Adm. O.: I think it was used as a museum and rest area for some of their workers. I don't know what, actually, other than that.

Q: The heating system was probably not very up-to-date, was it?

Adm. O.: Not very good, but then it was coming spring at that time, so that it wasn't too inadequate.

So, when I got down there everything was a horrible mess, but I got working with General Gorlinski, who was their senior man in charge of the reconstruction down there, and we made daily tours of all the buildings and the rooms and made lists of all the things which we felt were going to be needed -

furniture and equipment and things like that. We also had a member of the diplomatic staff, commissar, who was overseeing and trying to stick his nose into everything, and he did more to retard progress than anything else they could have sent down there -- Mr. Chavakin.

Q: Were all three delegations to be housed in the Livadia Palace?

Adm. O.: No. The British were to be elsewhere. The Russians were elsewhere, and this was only the American delegation and the meeting area. In the main building, we had to prepare a large meeting hall - that was the old ballroom. We had to prepare private rooms for the President and the senior members of his staff, and then in all the other rooms we had to prepare double-up bunks set military style row by row for generals and admirals on down. We had seven senior officers, I think, in one room. A little bit unheard of.

Q: Quite a number of stars, weren't there? Admiral King had the Czarina's boudoir, I think.

Adm. O.: He had his own space, of course. But this commissar came up at one time and insisted that he wanted the room right next to Roosevelt's room. I told him nothing doing, but he had been sent down by, he said, by Stalin to supervise this deal and for his own security reasons to protect the President he had to have the room next to his. I said I'm very sorry but we have a room reserved for you over here, and it was at the farthest corner on the second floor of the barracks and office building. I said that is where you and your two men are going to stay whether you like it or not. And he said, I'm going to stay down next to the President. I said, If you make a move to do that, I'm going to send a dispatch to Mr. Molotov immediately and have you recalled for interfering with the operations. At Molotov's name, of course, he blanched a little bit. So we finally compromised. He didn't want that room down there, he wanted the room over where I was going to put him.

Q: He saved his own face!

Adm. O.: Yes. Every night after we had made these tours of the buildings, a Russian convoy would set out over the peninsula, all over Yalta. They would scavenge from all the old buildings, the farmhouses, the schools, the hotels, any place that had furnishings, and pick up the things that we needed to fill our list and bring them in. The next morning I would see these things come in and unload and put into the rooms. When we got through, we not only had those buildings completely re-built and furnished, but planned with the allocation of all the officers who were coming - and, incidentally, by that time they had grown to 300...maximum number went up to 330!

Q: How many rooms were in this building?

Adm. O.: Oh, I don't remember, but we had them stuffed in like a barracks. We even had a barracks up on the third floor where all the guards and the enlisted men who came were lodged. We had two big restaurants - junior and senior ones - where they moved in all of the staff of the Hotel Splendide, the

Olsen - 35

National Hotel, and Moscow Hotel - the whole staff and all their equipment.

Q: From Moscow, they came down?

Adm. O.: From Moscow, to handle these two restaurants that we set up. Complete with Maitre D's, chefs, waiters, equipment and food and wines. The office building was separate. That was another problem because they couldn't understand why people couldn't work on their bunk or on a chair beside their bunk, why they needed an office. I had a hard time explaining to them why it was necessary, but we finally got all the offices laid out that we wanted. And the communication building, they had no place for that at all - that was the third building with the floors completely gutted out. So I went in and looked it all over and I said, "Well, if you'll get the planks - it doesn't have to be a finished job - if you'll just get planks and cover these big holes here and make the floor safe, we can arrange this." They were so relieved that I did not want a complete renovation that they agreed at once.

Now, going back a little bit, when I first got up there, we had arranged for the Catoctin, one of our communications ships, to come into the Black Sea with four minesweepers, and they came over to Sevastopol and tied up there. Immediately, after I'd visited them and told them what our requirements were, they sent a communications team in trucks over, and they laid land wires out over the 30 miles of land coming up to Yalta, and began to establish the communication link between Yalta and Sevastopol, and, of course, from Sevastopol back to the fleet. Until that time, we were talking by one little land wire between Sevastopol and Yalta on which I had to send all my coded dispatches down to them and then up to Moscow and answer back down there. I found nothing was coming through, so I made an early trip to Sevastopol and found they had them all stacked up while they were trying to break them down and analyze them before delivering them.

Q: I was going to ask about security with the Russians. I mean, how were you sure that you weren't...

Adm. O.: We had one of these single pad one-time codes that we rigged up ourselves. It was almost unbreakable unless you knew the book you were taking it out of. We were not concerned about that. What we were saying wasn't important anyway, but they just wanted to break it down and find out. I sent several in plain language because I wanted them to know.

Q: What about security in the rooms? I mean, you always hear about the Russians having devices of various kinds.

Adm. O.: Well, up in Moscow we knew perfectly well that they were taking advantage of every opportunity to set up hearing devices, even in the telephones. We were always conscious of this and were very careful about where and how we talked. I had an electrician up there who was briefed on all this equipment and we had him making inspections at Spasso House and the Embassy all the time. Actually, he pulled a listening device right out of the light up above the ambassador's desk in his own office, which shows how brazen they became in putting those things in. But down in Yalta with their people doing all the resurrection and so forth. We had no knowledge at any time of any activities such as that. We never found them, anyway.

Q: You were really vigilant!

Adm. O.: We were alert to it, but we never found anything and we had no reason to believe that they ever put anything in. Why, I don't know. Anyway, when we got this thing completed, we had the best first-class hotel in Russia, staffed by the best Russian staff available in Russia, as far as the restaurant facilities were concerned...

Q: For a week's stay...

Adm. O.: No, for two weeks. Our troops meanwhile, the people who were coming from Washington and so forth, had no idea what they were in for, and some of them came with a personal supply of C rations, a bed roll or a sleeping bag, and that sort of thing. They couldn't believe it when they found themselves set up in a first-class hotel, even though the living conditions were quite crowded. We, of course, had to establish our own security guards all around the place. The Russians had guards also around the place. Security, as far as the Russians were concerned, was very, very deep. The road was open between there and Sevastopol and we had daily convoys going over there bringing enlisted men over for their guard duty and supplies and that sort of thing. So, we were really pretty well fixed as far as our general living conditions were concerned. Much more so than the British. The British were out in another building and they came over and they couldn't believe that we had gotten as much as we got.

They asked how we got it. They wanted to move in with us.

Q: The Russians hadn't prepared for them?

Adm. O.: No. They wouldn't allow them much of anything. Stalin was in another broken-down castle and I don't think even he had as much as we had.

Q: It actually paid off in terms of results for the Russians. This probably was their intention.

Adm. O.: Yes, I think they were there to do everything they could to make our lives as pleasant as possible for this reason, to try to make it easy for Roosevelt. Roosevelt was a very sick man when he came over. As a matter of fact, when they had their first joint meeting in the big ballroom there, in the center of the room they had a big round table - you've probably seen pictures of it - with spaces for the Americans and for the British and the Russians. We were all in there and were asked to stay on the sidelines to line the two walls of the ballroom. The door was down here and the table was where that paper is. First Churchill came in the door and marched right down the center with his cigar, talking like this and the little bulldog look he always had. He was definitely on display, and he with his staff following, went and sat down. Then Roosevelt came in in his wheelchair with a big shawl over his shoulders and looking very, very tired and drawn, and this big Negro, Pleasant - I think that was his name - was pushing him. Of course, he was a great big burly, husky fellow, and this little old man looked like a little dried-up old lady sitting there, and he had to go through and was put into his other chair. And then Stalin came down, just glaring and looking as if he was expecting to have knives thrown at him at any minute from either side. But the contrast between the physical fitness of Churchill and Stalin versus Roosevelt was very, very striking. And, of course, all through the conference we had the feeling that Roosevelt was not holding up our interests to the best, that he was giving way, giving in to the Russians on almost everything. The comments made by Chip Bohlen when he came out sometimes indicated that that was what was going on.

Q: This couldn't have been prevented? I mean, his advisers couldn't restrain him from having a meeting at this point?

Adm. O.: Well, I don't know about restraining him from having a meeting, because he had that feeling all along, as he said and as was written up, I think, that his personality, his magnetism, was such that if he could talk personally with Stalin he could win a great deal more than he could by dispatch. I'm sure from all I have read that this was a strong personality complex with Roosevelt - that he had that feeling that he had to talk personally with Stalin, and that's why he wanted the conference.

Q: And Churchill was unable to deter things, apparently.

Adm. O.: I don't know what steps Churchill took, if any, to

delay the conference or to stall it. The British staff at one time earlier tried to break it up, but they were doing that on the basis that the airport at Simferopol was nothing but a great layer of mud and was not fit to bring planes in and out and they couldn't bring their people and materials in. That was passed on to me for comment, and I said, we made it, we had no problems, there was mud there but we got our gear all through, and there was no reason why they couldn't. So Harriman passed that on to Churchill, and Churchill just said, we go, just as quickly and bluntly as that.

As for the daily conferences and meetings, as I said before, I only administered and arranged the hourly details of housing and housekeeping and transportation, communications and so forth, but I took no part in any of the meetings, so I couldn't begin to discuss any of the results of that.

Q: They've all been reported in one way or another.

Adm. O.: They've all been hashed over so many times that I think that anything I said would be extraneous.

Q: I think the remarkable thing - I was reading this book The Yalta Conference with essays written by many of the people who were there, Hopkins and Byrnes, and Churchill, and Sherwood, Hudson, Hurley, Harriman, Gilmarx, Stettinius, Bohlen - and the remarkable thing is the divergence in the point of view as to what happened, and why it happened. Some of them diametrically opposite in their interpretation.

Adm. O.: I gathered that from what I've read, but I've not read this book or very much about it, actually. So I couldn't comment on the opinions.

Q: But one has the suspicion that back of it all was this key figure, Roosevelt, and his uncertain health.

Adm. O.: Yes. Hopkins, his main adviser, was not much stronger than Roosevelt, you know. Hopkins died - on the way home?

Q: He was in bed all the time, wasn't he?

Adm. O.: Yes, and Roosevelt died just a few weeks after he got home. In fact, I thought Roosevelt was going to pass out the night he spent on the Catoctin right after the conference, because - under darkened ship conditions and with the closed ports and everything, the cabin space was quite stuffy. I understand that he complained considerably and they opened the doors and ports but kept everything dark. But when we saw him on the field the next day going down the line in a jeep, as I say, he didn't look like he had long to live then. They told me that they were really scared in the Catoctin that he was not strong enough to go through with the trip. So I can't believe that a man in that physical status could be so strong-minded as to carry a point with people like Stalin and Churchill, and apparently he didn't.

Q: The irony is that the world has had to live with the decisions made.

Adm. O.: I don't know why they ever put Berlin in the triumvirate status in the middle of the Russian area, is something I could never understand. Why Churchill and Roosevelt ever agreed to that.

Q: One gathers from these accounts that Churchill didn't go along with a lot of this, but he simply had to when there were two against one, so he had to adjust.

One of your duties was also to act as an adviser on naval policy and matters to Ambassador Harriman. What did this entail? Can you cite illustrations?

Adm. O.: Very little, as a matter of fact. I merely kept advised myself, through the dispatches and the reports from the Navy Department that I got, as to what was going on in the Pacific. We had our weekly meetings at which I would discuss the Pacific war, its progress, and so forth, and Deane would cover the Atlantic side of things. We just had general discussions, general staff meetings, to keep everybody current with what was going on.

Q: Did you have a Moscow version of a war room?

Adm. O.: No. We had no such facilities. We did make a study, Deane and Spaulding, and myself, made a study of the capabilities of Russia to carry on the war in the Far East, and we pointed out to them that the one Siberian railway that they had was totally incapable of supporting a full-sized war over there without a tremendous stockpile in advance, and that the Russians were moving everything they could as fast as they could from the Western front to the Siberian front, even before the armistice, and that the Siberian railroad - every car, every flat car or anything that they could load was hauling stuff over there and moving troops over to be prepared when the day came that they could move. But, then, as you know, even after the armistice they stalled for a week before they admitted it, and then they were prepared and they went right down through China and took over all they wanted.

We had a plan, I mean we had a study of this and presented it to the ambassador.

Q: Was this study made in advance of Yalta?

Adm. O.: Oh, yes.

Q: So it was available to our people...?

Adm. O.: Oh, yes. They were quite aware of our analysis of the capacity of the railroad to support troops and equipment over there. But there was nothing they could do about it. Our people were planning to go on into Japan, as you know, and if the atomic bomb hadn't come along when it did we would have been faced with landings up there and that would have been very, very tough. So it was a good thing that that saved us from going in. The Russians meanwhile got what they wanted because they were planning for it and they didn't agree to the armistice until they had gotten a foothold and got what they wanted to out of it.

Q: Well, as you indicated earlier, in terms of certain Lend

Lease items, they were thinking always of postwar years and what they wanted, and they wanted territory as well as...

Adm. O.: Oh, yes. Of course, immediately the armistice was agreed upon, our Lend Lease pipeline stopped. It was full and it was agreed that we would not stop the flow of anything which had already been started to Russia, but that we would stop all future shipments, except for what was needed for reconstruction.

Q: What about ships for which the keels had been laid and were underway? Would they not get there?

Adm. O.: Oh, no. We would consign nothing after that. No, the pipeline stopped right there, but they let what was in the pipeline go on through. No, we didn't complete ships for them after that. The ships that we turned over to them were pretty limited anyway. A few merchantmen and the Milwaukee and some other small craft.

Q: And five minelayers!

Adm. O.: Five minelayers, yes! But of course that changed their attitude towards our Embassy people living over there, too. We were no longer much help to them and everything became very cold. When we pressed for various things we got the cold fishy eye after that.

Q: The cold war began right then?

Adm. O.: The cold war began immediately the armistice was

signed and our Lend Lease flow stopped. Then we were no longer of any use, and the people living in Moscow - I mean our people living in Moscow began to feel it very rapidly. They're strange people.

Q: What about social life as it involved Russians during your stay there? Was there very much of it?

Adm. O.: There was very little social life between us and the Russians. There were a few people, of course, a few of the younger men had liaison with some of the girls for dances, dinner parties, and things like that. Officially, we had almost none. Now, there was Admiral Stupanov, who was the deputy CNO, next to Kuznetsov. He was one of the few ex-Czarist officers who was still in service, still alive. He and I were very friendly in general conversation, and I invited him over to the house - to my apartment - a number of times but he always had to get permission to come. He couldn't get permission except when we had a cocktail party and there were a number of them, and then the main office designated how many and who would be permitted to attend. But he had a dinner for me one time and during the conversation, when we were side by side during dinner, he made apologies for the fact that he could not entertain me as I entertained him and his officers, but, he said, you know we live under very stringent circumstances. My wife and I have one room in an apartment building - he was the vice commander of the Navy and he had one room for him and his wife. He said, my wife works during the day but my office hours are practically all night, from mid-afternoon through until morning, so that when I go home my wife and I see each other for probably three hours during the day and that is all. He said, I have no facilities for entertaining and I can only entertain on an official occasion like this and then they grant me enough money and tell me that they want me to do this for diplomatic or political purposes. I hope you understand. This is not our personal feeling this is our official status. And I, of course, understood completely, but we never gave up trying to be sociable with them and invite them to our quarters. They came when they could, but as I say every time we issued an invitation they went through this screening apparatus and only certain people were allowed to come. Sometimes, they weren't allowed to come at all. That went on even at the Embassy. The Ambassador couldn't always have the people he wanted.

Q: Were the French at all present?

Adm. O.: No. The French were out. Their embassy was completely vacated. In fact, we got the use of their building for living quarters for our excess staff, and we used their chapel. We had a Catholic padre in there who got the use of their chapel while they weren't there. Also got the use of their wine cellar which I enjoyed on several occasions.

Q: Must have been lovely, yes. It's a wonder it remained there.

Adm. O.: When you have Napoleon brandy that's guaranteed to be something over 50 or 60 years old, it's pretty good.

There was just no social life between the people and ourselves. We would have a visit arranged to one of their farms - one of their ideal farms - or something. On those occasions we would be guided through everything, everything having been cleaned spic and span for us, and then we would be feted and fed. All the local people on the farm were very friendly, they wanted to talk about America and all about American life and so forth. They wouldn't believe half of what we told them because they couldn't believe that we had automobiles, and we all had electricity, that we had ice boxes and freezers, and radios and things like that. It got to the point sometimes where it was a little dangerous because they thought we were deliberately lying to them. You had to be a little careful just how much you told them. But, as I say, they were very friendly out in the country when we met them on a personal basis, not officially.

Q: Did you get out to some of officialdom's summer houses?

Adm. O.: No. Kuznetsov was going to invite me out there a couple of times, but he never did. He had a young wife and I think he was a little jealous of her and afraid that these young Americans might get too friendly. I gathered that because I made a comment, sort of a side comment, one time when, boy, did I get the cold fishy eye!

Q: My property!

Adm. O.: They invited us out to various events when they

could, sporting events and different parties, and, of course, they had their official parties in Molotov's building - big banquets and so forth - to which we were all invited. But, again, there was no personal contact.

Q: Did you get in the Kremlin at all?

Adm. O.: Oh, yes. We went in there a number of times, when they had some of their big dinners, big feasts. They were all grandiose affairs, much vodka, two and three courses of everything, and every two minutes or one minute there was a vodka toast to go down and somebody would have to get up and answer, that sort of thing. That was routine. All marvelous experience, but something you wouldn't want to go back and do over again.

Q: What was your impression of Harriman? How effective was he?

Adm. O.: He was a grand person, absolutely tops as a boss man. My only criticism would be that it took him a long time to make a decision. He usually would get the three of us - Deane, Spaulding, and myself - together and discuss a question at considerable length into the night. Once he had decided on what he was going to do, he wanted to wrap it up rather quickly and he'd call his stenographer in, a young lieutenant, Michaeljohn, and he would dictate to him a dispatch to go to the State Department. His dispatches usually took two, three, or four pages of typical State Department verbosity, and then we would sit down and talk about it. Then twenty minutes later he'd ring the bell for Michaeljohn and say, "Have you got that typed up yet?" Poor Michaeljohn would get all flustered. "Well, Mr. Ambassador, I just got it set up in my typewriter. I haven't had time to start yet."

Q: He may have been slow at decisions but he was quick in demanding service.

Adm. O.: Yes, indeed. I think he got along quite well with the Russians. They baited him all they could, but he probably didn't use the force and pressure that we would like to have seen him use on various occasions

Q: His immense wealth as a capitalist didn't stand in his way, then?

Adm. O.: I don;t think so. Of course, he never acted like a capitalist. He never carried a nickel in his pocket when he went out any place. If Michaeljohn wasn't around to pay the bills, we had to pay them. He didn't have his wife over there so it was slightly difficult for him at times. Kathy, his daughter, acted as his hostess and did a perfectly grand job, doing that as she could. But of course it would have been really much better if he'd had a wife there, I think, to run his house for him.

Q: Of course, it was wartime. I suppose it wasn't expected that there'd be much entertaining.

Adm. O.: No, true. But there was considerable at times though, just the same. Of course, when you went to the Russian quarters for entertainment, they never had their wives, at first. Now, that became a point a little later, because the Ambassador did have Kathy and the minister, George Kennan, when he came over, brought his wife with him, and some of the other nationalities all had their wives. So, all of a sudden, at some of the parties, the Russians finally got orders to bring their wives. The first party was not a very great success because the average Russian wife is rather a squat, dumpy, unintelligent, uncommunicative, and scared stiff type of person.

Q: Lacking social graces.

Adm. O.: Lacking any social grace. So you couldn't carry a conversation on with them. I think they got orders to review the situation and at the next party quite a different set of wives appeared! But, no, we never exchanged anything in the way of family life at all.

Q: How effective or how important, would you say, are the social gatherings when with the Russians it seems to be merely a facade?

Adm. O.: You mean while we were over there then?

Q: Yes.

Adm. O.: They were of no importance. It was just a return of courtesy to honor certain events, or certain days, certain occasions, and so forth, at which the big chiefs got up and made their national toasts, and a toast to the army and to the navy. Just an official front. It really served no get-together purpose.

Q: Did the Russian boys really enjoy this, however? Did they seem to?

Adm. O.: It was all free food and drink to them. Yes, they enjoyed it as far as they could hold their liquor. Molotov never took a drink on these occasions. He got called one time - I hope this isn't going in the Naval Institute, is it?

Q: No, no.

Adm. O.: It's just an amusing story. We were at one of these big affairs, and after the big assembly in the main ballroom with music and things like that, we went to three different rooms for the food and drink, and Molotov was going around with his batman right over his shoulder with his special carafe of vodka. Each time he'd run into a group he'd say hello to them and he'd have a toast. He'd hold his glass over to get it filled, and the boys would all pick up glasses of vodka from the table - carafes - and fill their glass, and then he'd say to the American Air Force" or whatever the occasion, "to the British fleet" or whatever it might be and he'd toss off his drink. One Air Force colonel was a little bit behind time on getting over to the table to get his filled, so he just grabbed the neck of the bottle that the batman was holding there - Molotov's - and poured it into his glass, and when the toast went up he took a drink and said,

Olsen - 52

"Good God, water!" Molotov disappeared! He was out in the next room.

Q: He was going to keep his faculties about him.

Adm. O.: Apparently, because he couldn't go from table to table and drink 30 or 40 toasts. But he was doing the honors.

Q: Maybe that practice was more general than one might suspect.

Adm. O.: As a whole, the Russians were not as capable drinkers as we give them credit for, because I think most of the Americans could outdrink the Russians at any of the banquets we had, as evidenced by the fact that it was usually the Russian who went under the table. I never saw an American go under the table. Even at Stalin's big banquets several of his generals would be under the table, would start falling down on his plate and so forth. The man next to him would give his feet a kick and his head a push and he'd slide under the table and he knew damn well he'd better not make any noise down there.

Q: A general under the table.

Adm. O.: Stalin commented to one of our visiting dignitaries over there that he didn't know what he was going to do with some of these generals, he'd better get some who could drink better. He himself didn't drink, you know. Nothing but a little Caucasian wine and that very mild. One time when

Churchill came in, and set up a dinner at the British Embassy. It was the only time that the British ever got Stalin into the British Embassy for a dinner party or for any reason. It was a very small affair, about 20 people at the inner sanctum. All the rest of us had been invited in for meeting Stalin and Churchill afterwards. We were all out in the main ballroom, stashed around the walls. We had to wait for about an hour and a half because Churchill was plying Stalin with stories and wine in there, in spite of the fact that he normally didn't drink. Churchill apparently had got him to drinking a little bit more than usual, and when they finally did come out they were both staggering a little bit. So we all closed in. Champagne was poured by the ushers all around the place, and Churchill and Stalin stood in front of the entrance to the dining room, and Churchill proposed a toast. They clicked their glasses and splashed their champagne all over each other! That's the only time I ever saw Stalin take enough to feel it. Of course, Churchill took it all the time. He had his brandy in one hand and cigar in the other.

Well, I think we've covered the waterfront pretty thoroughly.

Q: Yes, I thank you very much, Admiral, you've been very generous.

INDEX

Interview with

Rear Admiral Clarence E. Olsen, U. S. Navy (Ret.)

Allen, Ronnie, 31

Antonoff, General, 22

Berlin, 42

Bieri, VAdm. B. H., 2, 4

Bohlen, Charles E. (Chip), 39

Catoctin, USS communications ship, 35

Chase, Lt., 31

Chavakin, Russian Commissar, 33-34

Churchill, Rt. Hon. Winston S., 38-39, 40, 53

Cold war beginnings, 44

Communications: problems of for conference, 31, 35-36

Cooke, Admiral Charles M., Jr., 1

Deane, General, 3, 18, 42, 48

Duncan, Admiral Donald B., 2, 3, 5

Edwards, Adm. Richard S., 2

Eisenhower, General D. E., 22

Faymanville, General, 16

Frankel, RAdm. Sam B., 5, 7

Gorki, 17

Gorlinski, General (Russian), 32

Harriman, The Hon. Averill, 3, 5, 30, 40, 42, 48-49

Harriman, Miss Kitty, 49-50

Hill, General (A.F.), 31

Hopkins, Harry, 41

Kennan, The Hon. George, 50

King, Fleet Admiral E. J., 1, 33

Kremlin, 48

Kuznetsov, Admiral, CinC, Russian Navy, 14, 30, 47

Lease-Lend: 3, 13; request for minesweepers, 14-15; request for plans and specifications of naval ships, 15-16, 18; British Lease-Lend, 23, 44

Lividia Palace, 31-32; furnishings for conference, 34-35

Living conditions, for Americans in Russia, 25-26; for American prisoners, 27

Michaeljohn, 48-49 (Secretary to Ambassador Harriman)

Milwaukee, USS - turned over to Russia, 13-14, 44

Molotov, Russian Foreign Minister, 34, 51-52

Moscow, 2, 4

Murmansk, convoys, 5-6, 8, 10; condition of slave workers, 8-10

National Hotel, Moscow, 26

Oder River, 22-23

Odessa, possible meeting place for conference, 31

Olsen, Mrs. C. E., Letter to on Yalta Conference, 24; See also, appendix

Roosevelt, President F. D., 28, 29, 38, 39, 41

Roulard, Comdr., 11

Russia: study of Northern Passage to Murmansk, 1-2; travel conditions, 11-12

Russian Far East capabilities, study of, 42-43

Russian social life, 45-47, 48, 50

Russian suspicions, 19-20, 21, 22; dislike of British, 23-24, 30;
    restrictions on entertainment, 45-47

Security problems, 36-37

Sevastopol, 35-36

Simferopol Airport, 40

Spalding, General Sid, 16, 42, 48

Spasso House, 26, 28, 36

Stalin, Joseph, 28; refused to leave Russia for conference, 30,
    38-39, 52

Stalingrad, 16

Standley, Admiral William, 3, 5, 13

Stupanov, Admiral, Russian Deputy CNO, 45-46

Vladivostok, 11

Weather Information Exchange, Russia and U. S., 18-19

Yalta, 13, 30; transportation to, refused, 31; British accommoda-
    tions, 37-38

Yalta Conference, book of Essays, 40

www.ingramcontent.com/pod-product-compliance
Lightning Source LLC
Chambersburg PA
CBHW080609170426
43209CB00007B/1380